Antonio Montes Orozco

Scrum for Non-Techies

Learn how to use in your Business the methodology that led Google, Amazon, Facebook, Microsoft, and Lockheed Martin to success.

Table of Contents

Antonio Montes Orozco

Antonio Montes Orozco

Introduction

Scrum is a teamwork methodology for developing software and technology products. Starting in the 90s, nowadays is still the most used methodology in software development. Used by big companies such as Google, Amazon, Facebook, BBVA Compass Bank, Lockheed Martin, Microsoft, and many more, it helps in the creation of high-performance teams and group intelligence to fulfill any requested task.

Scrum is starting to expand in other environments that nothing have to do with software: schools, town halls, remodeling companies, strategical development plans for impoverished areas, and other several fields. All existing literature is focused on obtaining a software product, therefore, for non-techies, it might be complicated to hear about software terms such as unit tests, automated regression tests, TDD (Test Driven Development), pair programming or similar terms.

In this text I'll explain what Scrum is in a simple way, eliminating all the computer jargon. Hence I want you to be able to apply it in your environment, whatever it may be.

I hope reading this book helps you improve your Business efficiency and achieve success.

Antonio Montes Orozco

To

Rosa, the queen of my house, and my two princesses: Elena and Laura

Antonio Montes Orozco

Chapter 1: Some basic principles to take into account

In this chapter I am going to burn in your mindset some basics, so later on you can assimilate agile principles and Scrum reference framework better (we will talk about that later on).

1.1 Without involvement there is no commitment

Stephen Covey holds, in its work *Seven habits of Highly Effective People*, that without involvement there is no commitment (Covey, 2013). Commitment does not mean to obey, but to convert work into something of our own, in order to lead the way to the goal. **To** really **get involved** with something, **we must participate in the decision**. I can be told to do something, or how to do it, and even deadlines can be given to me but, if I didn't participate in the decision, my commitment level becomes null: that work will never be mine, it will not be my "baby". I'll fulfill it because of my professionalism and, in other cases, by other matters (getting fired, reprimanded, pay cut, etc.), but without a real commitment. If I see that something isn't going on well or can be improved, I won't say anything, since I'm not really committed: I'll stay quiet and let things follow its course, without doing my bit to help.

Therefore, **as a principle to save in our mindset, we must seek the involvement of the team in all decisions to be made**, so they can really commit with them. Whatever the Business, in the end you want to carry out a task through your teamwork. It's important that each member becomes really implicated. This commitment is achieved when everybody participates in the decisions.

In a democratic model, decisions are made by the majority. When majority decides, minority is not represented. In contrast, in an alignment model, everybody gives and adds to achieve the goal. This is an open context where everybody has the liberty and confidence to talk. The final decision does not represent a majority group, but everybody, since there has been an agreement. If everybody makes the decision, everybody is committed. Maybe a member of the team did not participate, if they had nothing to add, but they knew they had the liberty to do it, so the commitment remains firm.

Scrum is a methodology where full involvement is the key. That is why it works so well, since you get teams where each and every one of the members are committed with the Business.

To get some concepts ahead, I'd like to lay out how important it is to **create a confidence environment in a team**, so the members can feel with absolute liberty to show their ideas, and participate in rising discussions and decisions. The fear to participate and the lack of confidence will cause a non-debate, and therefore, a non-commitment team.

Commitment cannot be demanded. If employees are required to commit themselves, it doesn't work. We must make them part of the change. As leaders it is important that we understand this. What we have to do is to create a context so that workers can commit themselves to the business.

Antonio Montes Orozco

A leadership style that imposes decision, without taking into account the team´s opinions, cannot demand that employees overcome the project like something of their own. As Stephen Covey says in his book, underline this sentence: **<u>without involvement, there is no commitment</u>**.

1.2 Conflict is good and enriches the team

The word "conflict" has a negative meaning that makes us avoid it. In a professional environment, conflict appears when in a team there are several people with different opinions over the same topic, therefore it's always an open window to improvement. **Being able to view conflict as something positive and as an opportunity of learning and improving is a great advance in our mindset.**

If we see conflict as an opportunity to improve, we will stop avoiding it and we will face it in a constructive way. Once more, I emphasize how important it is for the team to create a confidence climate, so that conflict can appear in a natural way.

If we face a conflict from the classical negative perspective, we will face it with fear, in a defensive way, and possibly will get through it badly and with confrontations. If, on the contrary, we face the conflict with curiosity about how we are going to improve, we'll be more receptive to new ideas, listen and connect better with the faced parts and it'll be easier to reach an agreement.

When facing conflict, we can get some not-so-good comments about our performing. Our attitude has to be open to criticism and to self-criticism.

Antonio Montes Orozco

Only this way we will grow, mature and improve as persons and professionals.

If you are the type of people that panics over conflicts and doesn't see them as an opportunity to improve, probably you'll settle conflict from their cause, eliminating in your team the confidence to participate in discussions. In another chapter we will see how harmful this loss of participation confidence can affect the team. Finally, if you want to embrace Scrum methodology, you should be ready to see the team to come into conflict in a sincere and natural way, and admit criticism.

In all these years of experience with Scrum, I have always been enormously gratified to see teams **come into conflict in a healthy way.** Scrum suggests several types of meetings to create the context so that teams discuss and participate. I assure you that watching a team start an open, natural and full-of-confidence discussion, is one of the most gratifying pleasures in my professional life I have ever lived.

Therefore, in our leading style, we have to be open to criticism for a permanent improvement, and to accept conflicts with open arms.

1-3 The importance of trust in a team

Patrick Lencioni is an American writer (born in 1965) that wrote a business fable, *The Five Dysfunctions of a Team* (Lencioni, 2002), that describes the disastrous consequences of eliminating trust in a team.

Antonio Montes Orozco

Lencioni shows us that everything starts with the first dysfunction, that is the **absence of trust**. The leader of a team has the great responsibility of being their mentor. If they cannot recognize their mistakes, their team will not do it either, since the message they receive is "do not admit your mistakes". On the other hand, it may happen that, at anytime, someone has admitted to have made a mistake and the reaction of the team has been completely negative. Instead of supporting them, rewarding the shown trust and trying to solve the problem, their mates focus on avoiding their responsibility and smashing the guilty one. If, as a consequence of the previous reaction, a team member does not dare to recognize a mistake, they won't risk either to expose a new idea or participate in decisions. These kind of behaviors are the perfect breeding ground to plant the absence of trust.

When the team members cannot express themselves openly and trustfully, they tend to avoid conflict, so a false sensation of harmony appears. This is the second dysfunction mentioned by Lencioni: **fear of conflict**. Why am I going to express my opinion if they're going to disrespect me, despise me, not going to listen to me, or undertake reprisals against me?

If we are in an environment where we don't want to come into conflict and avoid it, the third dysfunction appears: **the lack of commitment**. Let us remember Stephen Covey's principle where he teaches us that without involvement there is no commitment. That is precisely what happens when avoiding to come into conflict: we do not participate in the decisions and, as a consequence, we are not engaged with our work.

Antonio Montes Orozco

When the team members are not engaged, the fourth dysfunction appears: the **avoidance of accountability**. Lencioni explains it to us as the lack of responsibility over the other team members. If any team mate breaks the rules or does anything wrong, we don't care, because we aren't engaged with the Business. We don't say anything and we look away. When we don't feel confident about coming into conflict, we don't compromise, and we avoid accountability, we don't care, including the results of the Business: we don't care whether it goes well or bad, because we are thinking about quitting, or being promoted to another department, or even changing to another company. This is the fifth and last dysfunction: **inattention to results**. At this point, little can be done. We will have to start from scratch, creating again the trust in the team. Let us remember that all this disastrous situation started when we destroyed the trust to participate. Let's record in our mindset that **it is vital to have trust inside the team: trust to participate and to make mistakes as well**. The first time that team members make a mistake, it is very important to be kind and not to smash them, as in that moment we will have destroyed their trust. As my grandmother used to say, only the one who cooks burns. In other words: it is normal to make mistakes at work. The one who doesn't work is the one that doesn't make them.

I especially like the analysis that Lencioni makes, because I consider that it synthesizes with wisdom the phases that a team destroying itself goes through. It is important to stay alert with this subject, as Scrum means teamwork. Always keep trust inside the team and stay alert with the slightest indication of loss of trust.

Antonio Montes Orozco

I had once a boss from whom I learnt a lot of good things. Every time that we made a mistake, he got into the middle and sent an e-mail, saying publicly that the mistake was due to him and that we had followed his instructions to the letter. He always remarked us that, with this policy, he took out from us the panic to make mistakes, so that we became more creative. And I assure you that it worked: we felt backed up and worked with more persistence. We were more creative and were not scared to put into practice the innovative ideas we had.

In all these years I have run into people that didn't know how to work as a team. It still strikes me when I see job vacancies where "teamwork" is asked. And how is this skill showed? There is no certificate that corroborates it. It is easy to say that someone is very good at team working, but a psychological test should be done to verify whether it's true that we know how to do it. Stay alert to the employees that do not know how to work as a team.

As you will be starting to see, these principles I am speaking about must be recorded in all and each one's mindset. They are principles that are learnt at childhood and that are transmitted from parents to children. We can acquire them at adulthood, but we need the will that makes us want to acquire them. A single individual that taunts their mates, or that is more aware of accusing their workmates than giving a solution to a problem, will destroy the trust in the team. You would get surprised of the damage that can be done by only one person. They are known as toxic people. Stay alert to detect the possible toxic members of your team. They must be halted as soon as they try to manipulate the team or destroy its trust.

Antonio Montes Orozco

1.4 Creativity is born out of relaxation. Avoid working overtime

Numerous scientific tests prove that, **when we are relaxed, our brain is in a more active and creative state**. To do so they connected electrodes to scientists while they were meditating (some Buddhist scientist has offered to do this test), checking, to the amazement of the assistants, how the activity of the brain increased (Ricard M., 2015).

The more productive creativity and brain activity are born from calmness and absence of stress. Thus, **if we want to find the solution to a problem, the most effective way is to relax and eliminate stress**. We will discover how our brain finds out the solution through the most imaginative possible ways.

In my life as a programmer, there were days in which I found myself with a problem at work and I did not know how to go on. I went back home and, to my wonder, I found out ideas when I was calmly relaxed and playing with my daughters. It was difficult to understand how in one minute a creative idea had occurred to me, which solved a problem I had been thinking about during hours at work. I had been stressed, pressed for delivery times and pressed by my boss. I learnt, in those days as a programmer, that I had to trust myself and that my creativity would appear when the appropriate conditions were given.

The subject of creativity goes much further than solving a programming problem. In any area of life a brilliant idea can save a lot of time and bring a lot of value to the Business. Hence, what do we win losing the opportunity of having a creative team? I imagine that you will be wondering where I want to go with this subject of the creativity; well, to a very controversial issue: overtime.

XP (Extreme Programming) is another agile methodology, like Scrum, and it explicates that not more than 40 hours per week must be done. Prolonging repeatedly our workday produces, not only physical and mental fatigue, but also some personal frustration. For most people it is not easy to get home and accept the idea that working for 10 hours has been the only thing they have done that day. Our *social being* rebels: we want to be with our partners, children, or just have a time for ourselves. We repeat ourselves the following idea: "I refuse to let my day be just this". But the clock alerts us to the harsh reality: the day has ended and it is the time to go to sleep. Sometimes we will comply, but other times frustration will take us to extend the day artificially, and our sleep will undoubtedly pay the consequences.

Science supports this measure with studies from 2015 about sleep (Stickgold, 2015). In those studies it has been discovered that the lack of sleep leads to three very harmful consequences for the human being:

1. We are more willing to get ill, as the lack of sleep affects our immune system.

2. It is easier for us to fall into depression, as the lack of sleep provoques, as a defense mechanism, that we remember just those negative things that have happened to us during the day. Imagine the mood you may have if you just remember negative things and there is nothing positive in your head. This accumulation of pessimism may lead us to a depression.

Antonio Montes Orozco

3. We tend to get fatter. The lack of sleep affects our endocrine system.

Imagine yourself in a period of stress at work, overtime and lack of sleep. You end up getting fatter, ill, and on the edge of depression. Besides, the extreme fatigue leads you to lose your creativity, so you try the same wrong ideas again and again, failing in your professional life. The extreme fatigue also leads us to make more mistakes. The mistakes reduce our productivity and may endanger our Business.

Agilism emerged to avoid triggering the previous process, which I call **work stress cycle**. I encourage you to be brave and get out of this vicious circle of stress. The signatories of the Agile Manifesto and Jeff Sutherland (he was also one of the signatories), inventor of Scrum, are contrary to these self-destructive working dynamics. Many countries engrave in the mindset of people that dedicating many hours to work is more productive and better. Well, it is just the opposite. There is an experiment of Jeff that I especially like: he realized that the work stress cycle was counterproductive, so he decided to reduce his workday. He discovered, to his amazement, that he had more creativity and he was more balanced, because he could dedicate time to his private life and, in short, he was more productive. Therefore, let's record in our mindset that **working overtime is counterproductive** and that we have to eliminate it from our teams, except in very exceptional cases.

Overtime can never be demanded from the team. It is the team that, on a voluntary basis, has to propose it to happen. Being aware of the counterproductive cost it has, we have to limit it, even when the team is very motivated and committed to doing so. Everything has consequences.

Antonio Montes Orozco

If you want to embrace the Scrum methodology, you must be willing to protect the team, preventing them from working unnecessary overtime.

1.5 Life is a path of continuous improvement

The Japanese have a term that I like very much: ***Kaizen***. **It means "continuous improvement"**. It consists of constantly assessing whether the process can be improved, looking for waste, or parts of the process that don't add value and can be eliminated. To do this, we must dedicate some time to stop and think about it. **Scrum prescribes a key meeting, which is the retrospective meeting**. In this meeting the team stops and reflects on what needs to be maintained, because it is working, and what things could be improved.

Throughout my life I have met many people who have seen this stopping and reflecting as a waste of time. They don't have faith that processes can be improved and they don't see the value of a team stopping to think. They don't see the value of stop working and going to a room to reflect. If they don't see the team stressed, staying in the office until very late, with dark circles and slovenly hair, it seems that they aren't being productive.

The Japanese apply *Kaizen* and you can't say precisely that they are unproductive. Imagine a team that thinks about how to improve every two weeks. In these reflections, action points emerge that are put to the test. Sometimes they will work and others the team will see that they don't add value. After three months, the team will have implemented six improvement actions; some will have meant an improvement, and the team will now be more productive. This is precisely what leads a **team** to have **high-performance**. These teams conquer the world and carry out any project.

To embrace the Scrum methodology, it is very important that you discover the value of stopping and reflecting, to improve and achieve virtuosity.

1.6 Summary

We have to record in our mindset the following principles, since they are the basis of Scrum and of teamwork, in general:

- **Without involvement there is no commitment**. Each time a decision is made, we must provoke all team members to intervene, to find the commitment. Recall that this principle is stated by Stephen Covey (Covey, 2013). We are not talking about making decisions democratically, but that each member of the team feels with the freedom and confidence to participate when they consider it appropriate.

- Let us dismiss the antiquated idea that entering into conflict is problematic. **Conflict enriches us** and encourages team members to participate, so it brings with it their commitment (thus returning to the principle enunciated by Stephen Covey**).**

- The absence of trust is the first dysfunction that can occur in a team, leading to other dysfunctions that will eventually destroy it. We must create an atmosphere of trust, where you can talk openly about any topic. We must always keep this point in mind, as it will serve as an indicator of the state of the team. Halt the toxic people of your team that undermine the confidence of your team mates.

- **Extending the workday leads to lack of sleep**, which in turn will affect our health. In such a state we lose creativity and make more mistakes at work, so **we lose productivity**. The loss of productivity **increases our stress**, entering more and more into the **work stress cycle**.

- **Doing overtime is counterproductive** and we have to eliminate it from our teams, except in very exceptional cases. If there is no other choice but to do so, the initiative must always start from the team and must be controlled to the maximum.

- **Life is a path of continuous improvement**. Learn to see the value of stopping and reflecting on what things can be improved, and what is working well and must be maintained.

Chapter 2: A little of philosophy

We've seen a series of basic principles associated with the team management and its operating. Now I would like to deepen into how we appreciate the individual. What philosophical vision do we have of the rest of human beings? Do we trust them? What needs do our colleagues have? What leadership styles suit best the principles and values of Scrum?

2.1 Maslow's Hierarchy of Needs

Abraham Maslow was a twentieth-century American psychologist. He was born in Brooklyn, New York, in 1908, and died in Palo Alto, California, in 1970. He was one of the founders of humanistic psychology, and what interests us is his theory about the needs of human beings, starting with the most basic one to achieve personal self-actualization. He sustained that human beings tended, in the first place, to satisfy their most basic physiological needs: eating, drinking, sleeping, breathing, having sex...

Only when these basic needs were achieved, human beings began to think about the needs of the next level: safety needs. These needs have to do with having job security, not breaking the family unit, having some security in health, or the moral of the environment, or that resources are not going to be exhausted. In short, everything that leads us to feel secure and protected.

The next level is the need for belongingness and love. This need is formed by our self-esteem and the esteem that others have for us. The first thing is to love ourselves and, afterwards, that others also love us. When this need isn't covered, we find ourselves with low self-esteem. We all want to be that successful person we have dreamed of. Without covering this need, we feel doomed to failure and cannot achieve anything by our own means.

But we need more. The last level would be the need for self-actualization. It does not make sense to speak of self-actualization if some lower level has not been covered yet.

And why do I tell you all this and what is the use of knowing Maslow's Hierarchy of Needs? Because, philosophically speaking, how we perceive others will determine our style of leading. If we think that other people only try to cover their physiological needs, we tend to think that they don't like to work and that they don't want to assume responsibilities. Would you trust people who don't like to work nor take responsibility? It is hard to trust a team with that appreciation, so our leadership style will tend to be dictatorial.

If, on the other hand, we see others as beings who also have social and recognition needs, we will understand that they like to work and assume responsibilities. Therefore, our leadership style will delegate more responsibilities to our collaborators.

And, furthermore, if we assume that the purpose of every worker is self-actualization, we will understand, naturally, that they will be willing for us to delegate to them and give them confidence.

Antonio Montes Orozco

Levels	Human Being Needs
Physiological needs	Food, water, warmth, rest.
Safety needs	Physical security, employment security, resource security, moral security, family safety, health security, private property security.
Belongingness and love needs	Intimate relationships, friends.
Esteem needs	Prestige and feeling of accomplishment.
Self-actualization	Achieving one's full potential, including creative activities.

Let's have a look at the leadership styles that flow out from the perception we have of our neighbor.

2.2 Leadership Styles

Douglas McGregor was a twentieth-century American economist. He was born in Detroit, in 1906 and died in 1964. He claimed two theories on leadership, called Theory X and Theory Y (McGregor, 2006). Both theories are closely related to Maslow's Hierarchy of Needs, since they emanate from the perception that the leader has of the leaded personnel.

Antonio Montes Orozco

Theory X (Dictator vs. subordinate)

Theory X emanates from the perception of the employee as a person who only tends to cover physical needs and, therefore, who doesn't like to work or commit. This leads to the belief that the only way to dominate the employee is through threat and punishment. Scrum cannot be applied with this vision of work colleagues. Theory X needs strong hierarchical structures, where there is always a supervisor for each employee. Threat and punishment eliminate employee's confidence to participate in decisions, eliminating the commitment of the members of a team (let's remember Stephen Covey and his principle that without involvement there is no commitment). Similarly, by eliminating the confidence of the team, this will enter into dysfunction (let's remember the five dysfunctions of the teams that Lencioni talked about), so in the end we will have a team that doesn't attend the results and where there will be a high turnover.

Theory Y (Coordinator vs. collaborators)

The Theory Y parts of the understanding that employees need to meet their esteem and social needs, so the leader understands that the employee likes to work and take responsibility. Theory Y considers the employee as the most important asset of the company. There is no full trust in them, but it is understood that they can solve problems creatively. It's a great advance with respect to Theory X, but under Theory Y Scrum is not allowed, because it is necessary to advance one more step towards the following theory.

Theory Z (facilitator leader vs. team)

We jump from Douglas to William Ouchi, an American professor born in Honolulu (Hawaii), in 1943. Ouchi had the opportunity to get to know the Japanese business world and was able to compare the various leadership styles between American and Japanese companies. Theory Z focuses on giving the employee a stable working environment for life and in seeking fidelity, caring for their well-being, both inside and outside of work. The high moral and employee satisfaction leads to high productivity. With Theory Z, leaders consider that the employees need to reconcile their professional life with their private life, apart from self-actualization. Having happy employees makes it possible to deliver full confidence in them. With this confidence the employee yields to the maximum and behaves as expected. That is why the Z leader says "what" but the employee decides "how": empowerment is given to the team to decide how things are to be done. The leader Z is a facilitator of the team. They are also known as the **servant leaders**, since they will eliminate the obstacles the team could be encountering. In accordance with the above principles, Theory Z is the one that best suits Scrum, because it empowers the team (the team itself decides how to work) and creates a context of trust, essential for the team to be able to commit.

2.3 Summary

- The human being has needs, some more basic than others. Satisfying a level of needs opens our minds to the next level. That means that it isn't enough to have a pay raise, or a stable job. Sooner or later we will want more. And so on until achieving self-actualization, which is the maximum expression of our potential.

- The appreciation that we have of the employees will determine our style of leadership.

- Theory X understands that employees only have physiological needs, hence they don't like to work and you have to use threat and punishment with them.

- Theory Y understands that employees also have social and esteem needs, hence they like to work and assume responsibilities. The leader Y delegates more to their cooperators.

- Theory Z understands that employees tend to self-actualization, so the Z leader is concerned about employees' is happiness and balance, both inside and outside of work. The Z leader is a facilitator and eliminates the obstacles the team finds. They are also called servant leaders, because they are at the service of the team. The team is empowered to decide how to do things.

Chapter 3: A little of history

3.1 Jeff Sutherland

While in the 1960s workers suffered from the tyranny of the X chiefs and the rigid and inflexible working methods, Jeff Sutherland, the inventor of Scrum, was engaged in piloting combat aircrafts in the Vietnam War. Jeff, during this time in the army, burned into his mindset the following values:

- The value of **trust** in the team, because otherwise you were dead.

- The value of **self-organized and multidisciplinary** teams. Jeff was used to seeing fully autonomous special mission commands that contained a doctor, a sniper, an interpreter, an explosives expert, etc. These commands could undertake any type of mission, because they contained all the necessary specialists to carry it out. They were given the vision of what it was needed to be done, they self-organized and acted autonomously.

- The value of the **continuous inspection**. Jeff met a fighter pilot instructor who was the best in his category. This instructor was obsessed with the **OODA** principle, which consisted in **Observing, Orienting, Deciding and Acting**. First the situation was observed by pilots, then they were oriented towards an objective, then the tactics to be followed were decided and, finally, action was taken. This simple principle is what caused American fighters to have far fewer casualties than Russian MIG fighters, piloted by Koreans and Vietnamese, despite the fact that Russian aircrafts (MIG) were faster and more maneuverable. The cause of this fact was slow to meet. In the end they realized that the key was that the American pilots had more visibility from their cockpits than the Vietnamese or Korean pilots, so they could apply OODA iteratively. The Americans saw their enemies before, oriented their attack, decided a tactic and acted. Then they repeated the process again, iteratively, while the Vietnamese, shorter and in large cockpits (prepared for Russian pilots, who were taller), did not know where the attacks came from, so they couldn't practice OODA, as they couldn't observe the situation.

Upon returning from the front, Jeff graduated in statistics from Stanford University and went to work in the University Laboratory of Artificial Intelligence. From there he went on to teach mathematics in the Air Force. Then he did a course in Bio-Measurements at the Medical School of Colorado, and received his doctorate in Bio-Measurements. All this effort made him realize that human communities are complex adaptive systems, as cell communities are. Every time you try to change an organization, people get lost and become resistant to change, but then everything comes to an equilibrium, just as it happens to cells.

The Reagan Administration made a major cut in the research, so Jeff was laid off and had to change area. He was hired by MidContinent, a software company that valued his knowledge in statistics.

There Jeff found himself with an environment X of the 70s, where people were treated disrespectfully, there was no trust and where a lot of time was spent executing unproductive tasks. Jeff, who had experienced the value of trust in the team, came across dysfunctional teams, where members didn't involve in the decisions, so they couldn't commit to them.

Antonio Montes Orozco

Neither was the context created towards Observe, Orient, Decide and Act (OODA, you remember?). In contrast, an initial plan was set and the project was sticking to that plan with earmuffs, as if the plan was more important than the response to the change.

And, to Jeff's astonishment, he saw how the specialists trenched themselves into hindered departments and communicated with the rest of the world through documentation, being insensitive to the project and unaware to the commitment to move it forward. The teams couldn't carry out the projects themselves, so they required the collaboration of those hindered departments that I mentioned. The result was projects that got stuck because of the internal bureaucracy of the companies.

Thanks to the excellence that Jeff showed, he got a position as vice president at MidContinent, so he was able to test a change plan. Together with his collaborators, he designed a new methodology that applied all the values and principles that he had brought from the war. That methodology made a lot of emphasis on teamwork, so they gave it the name of **Scrum** (*mêlée*, in French), which is the phase of rugby where players come together to design the game strategy. Other privileged minds detected the same problems and devised ways to develop software in a more efficient way, such as Kent Beck, who devised Extreme Programming, known as **XP**. Jeff, Kent and other software gurus drafted the Agile Manifesto, the starting point of the agile revolution, which restored values to the business world.

Antonio Montes Orozco

3.2 The Agile Manifesto

The Agile Manifesto was written by Jeff Sutherland along with Martin Fowler, Ken Schwaber, Kent Beck and other brilliant minds of the time. It's true that all of them came from the software world, and it's also true that the title of this book is "Scrum for Non-Techies", but we have to give the software world the origin of this teamwork methodology. What many software companies experienced in the 90s was a true chaos:

- Unmotivated teams.

- Projects that didn't end. Not finishing a project meant that it had been delayed twice as much as estimated, or cost twice as much as budgeted.

- Projects that didn't deliver what the client requested.

- Money loss, use of great efforts in completely unproductive tasks that did not add any value.

That is precisely the scenario that both Jeff and the rest of the signatories of the Agile Manifesto found. This group of visionaries met, on February 17, 2001, in Snowbird, Utah, to try to put common sense to this situation.

The Agile Manifesto they wrote is a compendium of four values and twelve principles, and they constitute the support of agile methodologies. Any methodology that applies these values and principles is an agile methodology. Scrum applies them, so Scrum is one of the agile methodologies that exist (XP, mentioned above, would be another one). And how are the values of the principles different? "Values" are a moral code, while "principles" are laws or rules that are followed to achieve a purpose. For example, all thieves lack principles, because they don't follow the law or rule of respecting the property of others. However, even thieves have values, because they follow the moral code of not stealing from each other.

Scrum is based on agile values and principles, and we'll see them in detail in the following chapters.

Chapter 4: Values followed by Scrum

Scrum is an agile framework so, like any methodology of this type, it is based on the four values defined in the Agile Manifesto. Remember that, as stated in chapter 2, values are a moral code. Below I quote the fragment of the Agile Manifesto, where the four agile values are defined:

"*We are uncovering better ways of developing software by doing it and helping others do it. Through this work we have come to value:*

- Individuals and interactions over processes and tools.

- Working software over comprehensive documentation.

- Client collaboration over contract negotiation.

- Responding to change over following a plan.

That is, while there is value in the items on the right, we value the items on the left more."

The four Values are very much oriented to create software products, but these values are equally valid for any other environment. Therefore, I am going to reformulate the four agile values as follows:

- Value individuals and their interaction more than processes and tools.

- Prefer the result that adds value to the exhaustive documentation.

- Value client collaboration more than contract negotiation.

- Value more the response to change than following a plan.

Antonio Montes Orozco

I explain in detail what implications each of the four agile values have.

4.1 Value individuals and their interaction more than processes and tools

Processes facilitate work and are an operational guide. They must be adapted to Organization, teams and people; and not the other way around.

Tools improve efficiency. But the results come thanks to people's knowledge and their attitude. Therefore, this value puts the focus on people, with priority over processes and tools.

The business theory of the 90s postulates that very well-crafted processes can achieve extraordinary results with mediocre people. In this approach you can guess the lack of confidence in people at that time, trying to substitute the low concept of them through rigid procedures. Nowadays, almost all businesses have an important creative and innovative component. Putting the focus on the processes and forgetting about people can make us less competitive. If your Business does not require any creativity or innovation and a well-structured process is enough, Scrum may not be for you.

To illustrate this value moreover, I will give you an example: how many times have I seen the absurdity of sending an email to the partner next to us, when it is much more efficient to get up and talk to them? I've seen an email being sent to the companion sitting right in front of them, just to ask them if they planned to attend a meeting. The mail is bundled, because the partner didn't understand what meeting it was. In the end the emails get

Antonio Montes Orozco

complicated and the companions end getting up to clarify that it was the quarterly results meeting. But of course, all this takes place two hours after the first email started, when with a simple face-to-face question everything would have been cleared up in five minutes. Other times I've found extensive emails, so boring that you don't even know what to do with them. You read them, you don't understand anything and, at the end of the week, I ask them how X procedure is done. They reply, offended, that everything was in the mail: in that email sent a week ago with no way to handle it. It is clear that face to face is the most efficient form of communication, because it gives us much more detail than a cold mail: tone of voice, gestures, body language, etc.

Through the tools and procedures we lose a lot of information and don't communicate efficiently. I remember once that I needed a department to do a small task for my team. For this, instead of face-to-face, they had a procedure based on the use of a tool to create the request via filling a form. I used the tool, but it was so complex that I didn't fill in a field of the form correctly. The person who answered my request, instead of calling me by phone to obtain the missing information, rejected the request in the tool. For that person my project wasn't something important, so they left my team on hold for weeks. If they had called me on the phone, I would have given them the information that was missing and my team would have been working without interruption. How much did it cost to the company having a team of 8 people on hold for several weeks? How many millions of dollars are lost daily in complex processes and lack of communication, in favor of complex tools to be used? **Focusing on procedures and tools**

Antonio Montes Orozco

makes us less competitive, as it stands in the way of communication among professionals.

4.2 Prefer the result that adds value to the exhaustive documentation

This point affects delivering something that brings value as soon as possible. If we quickly deliver the minimum version that adds value, the client can see it and give us their opinion. With this opinion, we feed the process and bring the final result closer to what they really want. Many times the client doesn't know what they want, or specifies it wrongly. With an early delivery of "something that adds value", the client clarifies ideas and specifies what they want better. The requirement's documentation that is generated at the beginning of a project will never approach the final result. Therefore, why are we going to invest time in something that is going to change for sure, and from which we do not have enough data?

The Manifesto doesn't affirm that it isn't necessary. The documents allow the knowledge transfer, record historical information and, in many legal or regulatory matters, are mandatory, but emphasizing that they are less important than the result that provides value.

Therefore, we must run away from the documentation that doesn't really add value. In addition, we must erase from our mindset the idea that a document can replace the valuable communication that is established between two people talking face to face.

Antonio Montes Orozco

If the organization and the teams communicate through documents, there is a risk that this documentation will be used defensively as barricades faced with departments or individuals. Department A does not respond to the request of Department B, since the TP20 form has not been properly filled out (I just invented this type of form). Now the TP20 has a green cover. They will not attend the request until they get the green cover. Is there no green paper? Well, we'll have to wait a week until the material order arrives and the TP20 can be delivered with green cover. Meanwhile, Department A sits back, doing nothing, and Department B pulls its hair out. But filling in the TP20 is of the utmost importance. That is what I mean by using documentation as a barricade between departments.

4.3 Value client collaboration more than contract negotiation

In agile methodologies, the client is a member of the team, who integrates and collaborates with it. A contract can leave untreated aspects that are important for the client. To stop contributing value to a client, because it is not in the contract, is the opposite of collaborating together.

The client doesn't have to be an expert defining what they want and may not even have a clear idea of what they want. But contracts are signed at the beginning of the client-supplier relationship. Are you going to stop giving a good client service because it was not accurately reflected in a contract? For Agilism, close cooperation with the client is vital. Therefore, contracts are very generic, and what a client is buying is time. During this time, the supplier makes early deliveries to the client, which provide value.

Antonio Montes Orozco

In this way, the client can clarify ideas and give the supplier feedback on what is delivered. With this methodology there is certainty that what is delivered will be what gives more value to the client and what they really want.

The contract between both parties is necessary. It is a formality that must be fulfilled, but Agilism doesn't use it to establish dividing lines between responsibilities. From the first moment the client is part of the teamwork and the relationship is of close collaboration.

4.4 Value more the response to change than following a plan

Be the Digital Bank Acme bank. This bank wants to digitize itself and designs a plan to incorporate the following functionalities to the mobile and web application: balance accounts, movements, make transfers, create a new account, hire a car insurance. The plan is fixed and software development begins. It is expected that, in a year, the bank will be able to have its two digital media (mobile and web application) completed with all the functionality established in the plan. But, two months after starting, Competitor Bank launches functionality that is very well received by its customers: the payment through mobile and instant deactivation of cards from their mobile, to avoid embezzlement in the event of the loss of a card. The CEO of the bank pulls their hairs on despair, seeing that their plan has already been outdated and that the mobile payment functionality was not included in it. Digital Bank Acme will lose a golden opportunity to be in the big banks league and will be in the second row, like a technologically outdated bank. The plan is ongoing and, for a year, mobile payment development cannot begin.

The desperation of the CEO of Digital Bank Acme comes from the rigidity of the plans. They have lost a Business opportunity to position the company in the market, along with the big competitors. If they had applied agile methodologies, mobile payment would have been included in the middle of the development of the applications and, in a short time, Digital Bank Acme would already have its payment by mobile, just like its competitors. It could even have overtaken some of them and now it would have a leading position in the market.

The prefixed plans are necessary, but they don't take advantage of the opportunities presented in between. The market is flexible and constantly changing. We cannot lose an opportunity that occurs because it does not fit a predetermined plan. Agilism values more the response to change, to take advantage of these opportunities, position the company better against competitors and maximize the return on investment.

Antonio Montes Orozco

4.5 Summary

The four points of the moral code that governs Scrum are the same as those governing any agile methodology, and they are the following:

1. Value individuals and their interaction more than processes and tools.

2. Prefer the result that adds value to the exhaustive documentation.

3. Value client collaboration more than contract negotiation.

4. Value more the response to change than following a plan.

Chapter 5: Principles followed by Scrum

The Agile Manifesto contemplates, in addition to the four values which Agilism is based on, twelve principles. Remember that principles are laws or rules that are followed to achieve a purpose. The twelve principles of the Agile Manifesto say literally the following:

"*We follow these principles:*

1. Our highest priority is to satisfy the customer through early and continuous delivery of valuable software.

2. Welcome changing requirements, even late in development. Agile processes harness change for the customer's competitive advantage.

3. Deliver working software frequently, from a couple of weeks to a couple of months, with a preference to the shorter timescale.

4. Business people and developers must work together daily throughout the project.

5. Build projects around motivated individuals. Give them the environment and support they need, and trust them to get the job done.

6. The most efficient and effective method of conveying information to and within a development team is face-to-face conversation.

7. Working software is the primary measure of progress.

8. Agile processes promote sustainable development. The sponsors, developers, and users should be able to maintain a constant pace indefinitely.

9. Continuous attention to technical excellence and good design enhances agility.

10. Simplicity —the art of maximizing the amount of work not done— is essential.

11. The best architectures, requirements, and designs emerge from self-organizing teams.

12. At regular intervals, the team reflects on how to become more effective, then tunes and adjusts its behavior accordingly."

The agile principles are guided to the software production, so we can see in the writing the repetition of terms related to software development. To explain these principles in an understandable way, I turn them into the following:

1. Satisfying the client, delivering value as soon as possible.

2. Accept the change in requirements, whenever they come.

3. Deliver value frequently.

4. Work side by side with the client.

5. Work with motivated teams.

Antonio Montes Orozco

6. Search face to face communication.

7. Measure progress for what is delivered.

8. Maintain a sustainable work pace.

9. Try to be very good at what we do.

10. Minimize waste and work that doesn't add value.

11. Allow the team to self-organize in order to obtain the best results.

12. Reflect on our successes and failures.

I will then describe each of them in detail.

5.1 Satisfying the client, delivering value as soon as possible

If we don't show the client any results until the end, we may come as a great surprise that what we give them is not what they expected. In addition, clients often don't know exactly what they want. Only when they see something is when they begin to clarify ideas and refine their requirements.

This principle is valid for all types of businesses: delivering something that provides value ASAP, so that the client sees it and gives us feedback.

If you remember the principle of OODA (Orienting, Observing, Deciding and Acting) that Jeff Sutherland learned in Vietnam, this rule is very much related to repeating this process as much as possible. That's why it is important that we deliver value ASAP, precisely because the client gives us feedback very soon and we can adjust our work without losing precious time. This will lead us to success.

5.2 Accept the change in the requirements, whenever they come

Agile methodologies adapt to changes very well. Without defined plans to be followed strictly, you can make changes at any time. Let us imagine that we are applying Scrum to a company that conducts financial studies. This iteration is analyzing the evolution of the main European stock indexes, and the next iteration analyzes the implications of the incentives that the European Central Bank applies to the European economy. But in between, Great Britain decides to leave the European Union, reason why it's urgent to analyze the repercussions that the Brexit can have (denomination to the exit of Great Britain from the European Union). Well, the task of preparing a report on Brexit is introduced and it's prioritized over the one that had been planned on the evolution of European stock indexes. This is the advantage of not following a strict and unchanging plan: we can always be adapted to changes to gain benefit of market developments and opportunities.

5.3 Deliver value frequently

Going back to the beginning of the OODA, the more we inspect what we're doing and the more we deliver value, the more feedback we get from the client, so we will get closer to the final result desired. If, for example, we don't deliver value within a year, we may find that it is not what the client expects. In that case, we would have been wasting time and money, and it'd be time to start over. The delivery of value in Scrum is iterative and incremental:

- **Iterative**, because we don't do everything at once, but we work during an iteration, stop, observe, adjust and iterate again.

- **Incremental**, because we contribute value little by little and never at once. The result comes iteration after iteration, all to apply the OODA principle.

5.4 Work side by side with the client

As a basic rule, we must collaborate with the client as much as possible. Therefore, the client is represented in the team through the role of **Product Owner**, as we'll see later on. In fact, we'll see that, after each iteration, the result will be shown to the client, so they can tell us if what is presented fits what they want. Let us recall the value of the Agile Manifesto that gave priority to collaborate with the client against limiting the relationship to a contractual agreement.

5.5 Work with motivated teams

A very fashionable phrase is that employees are the most important asset of companies. Scrum takes this phrase to the ultimate consequences, ensuring that team members are really happy and motivated. If you remember Theory Z, where employees were taken care of and delegated to them, in Scrum it becomes totally true. Even in XP, another agile methodology, a maximum of 40 hours a week is regulated, so that team members do not "get burn" and have a balance between their personal life and their professional life. With this quality of life, turnover in the team is minimized. Turnover occurs when people resign and go to another company, taking their knowledge with them. The loss of experience does a lot of damage to the teams. Scrum minimizes the turnover taking care of the team and getting them to achieve self-actualization, as explained by Maslow in his famous Hierarchy of Needs (chapter 2).

A motivated team enters a virtuous cycle of continuous improvement, where the team matures every day and where everyone participates, reaching full commitment.

5.6 Search face to face communication

We tend many times to send emails or communicate through tools. Such communication is ineffective and lends itself to misunderstandings. Whenever we can, let us try to communicate face to face. I remember a colleague who liked to use emails and tools instead of face-to-face. That created tremendous communication problems, because sometimes I did not understand what he wanted to say and he believed that, having used the tool or having sent the mail, the message was already transmitted.

To communicate effectively we have to be sure that they understand what we have transmitted and that the recipient of the message has listened to what we have communicated. Neither an email nor a tool can assure us anything of this. You would be surprised at the number of professionals who have hundreds of unread emails in their inbox. The same thing happens with the tools: if I am not connected to the tool, it'll be difficult for me to find out about the changes or notifications that have occurred. And although I have managed to read the email, I am not always with the degree of concentration required by certain emails, especially if they are especially long. Face-to-face eliminates any obstacle in communication.

The next time you have to communicate, think first of face-to-face, you'll see how much it improves your communication.

5.7 Measure progress for what is delivered

In classical project monitoring methodology, metrics are created to determine the progress of the project. These metrics are expensive to calculate. It is another example of waste. It is more direct to see what has been delivered, since all deliveries add value to the Business. For example, if our product is a car, if we observe that the chassis has been delivered with the engine and the bodywork, and we see that the seats and the electrical installation are missing for the following deliveries, it gives us a clear idea of how the project is going. We know we have a car that works and that only touch-ups are needed. This is because we have followed the methodology of cutting the project into tasks that add value for themselves. If the tasks did not add value to the Business, it would not be so easy to measure the progress, since the deliveries would not tell us anything. Therefore it is important that we learn to chop the work to be done in tasks that add value to the Business.

5.8 Maintain a sustainable work pace

A team doing overtime can get a job ahead, but for how long can it maintain that pace? Remember what I call the "work stress cycle": overtime leads to being late at home; being late leads to stealing hours of sleep in our lives to do "something other than work"; lack of sleep leads to physical and psychological consequences that reduce our productivity. But, if we find a sustainable work rhythm, we will be productive indefinitely.

There is an exercise that I especially like, and consists of assembling several teams of two people each. In each team, one has to clap and the other has to count. The team that gives the most number of palms wins. The members of each team decide when they exchange in the work of clapping. The usual thing is that they start clapping very quickly, but soon the tiredness appears and the joints begin to hurt. The teams discover that this is not a sustainable rhythm. In the end, the teams end up clapping slowly, reaching a sustainable rhythm that does not cause pain in the joints. Remember what we saw in chapter 1, where I explained that creativity was born of relaxation and that overtime had to be avoided. Making intense efforts is not sustainable and in the long term brings problems. Therefore, we must take care of the team and ensure that they reach a sustainable rhythm, so that they become productive indefinitely and always creative.

5.9 Try to be very good at what we do

The purpose is to assemble a high-performance team whose members have a great talent. Employees are the most important asset of the companies and Scrum keeps this always in mind, as well as any agile methodology.

A team of high-performance, committed and with highly talented members does the same job in half the time.

There is a blunt phrase that reads: "Scrum is not for mediocre". It looks for talent, high-performance, sustainable pace, stability in the team, a job well done. In agile methodologies such as XP, work is even prescribed in pairs, so that the knowledge is spread by the team and, in the end, they end up doing everything, minimizing the damage caused by the resignation of the staff. Although work in pairs is typical of software environments, I encourage you to try it in your environment, even if it has nothing to do with the software world. When working in pairs, one puts in command of the computer and the other looks. With this, the transmission of knowledge by the team is achieved, since the couples are rotating and, in a short time, everyone has been with everyone. The work in pairs also achieves a higher quality in what has been done, as four eyes see more than two. The usual values lead us to think that working in pairs does not take advantage of the resources, because you have two people doing the work of one. But empirically it is demonstrated that it is more efficient, because the work comes out faster and without errors. Have the courage to change paradigms and try new things. Reality shows that this works, even if logic says otherwise.

5.10 Minimize waste and work that does not add value

Agile methodologies place special emphasis on not wasting time on tasks that do not add value. For example, to establish a procedure that forces teams to generate the TP20 (fictional document that I just invented), when this document is always outdated and does not really serve at all, it is a waste of time that does not add value. You have to avoid this type of tasks. How many millions of dollars are lost per year in tasks of this kind? This may seem like a truism, but you would be surprised at the amount of time and money lost in companies performing tasks that do not add value.

5.11 Allow the team to self-organize in order to obtain the best results

If you remember Theory Z, in the end the key was to give confidence to the team and empower it, so that it decided how to perform the tasks. The leader communicated the vision (what had to be done), but the team decided how. Therefore, the team self-organizes, obtaining its maximum potential. The team decides and participates in all decisions, so that its degree of commitment is maximum.

Antonio Montes Orozco

5.12 Reflect on our successes and failures

Do you remember the continuous improvement, summarized by the Japanese word *Kaizen*? Periodically the team meets to reflect on how it can improve. Imagine a team that makes this reflection every two weeks. After reflection, corrective actions are proposed that are carried out during the following weeks. In the following reflection, new topics are addressed and the proposed corrective actions are reviewed. After a month, two groups of corrective actions have been undertaken; after a year, the way of working of the team has gone through successive processes of refinement (about twenty-six), so the team is already a high-performance team that works with the precision of a clock.

5.13 Summary

The 12 laws (or principles) that govern agile methodologies are the following:

1. Satisfying the client delivering value as soon as possible.

2. Accept the change in requirements, whenever they come.

3. Deliver value frequently.

4. Work side by side with the client.

5. Work with motivated teams.

6. Search face to face communication.

Antonio Montes Orozco

7. Measure progress for what is delivered.

8. Maintain a sustainable work pace.

9. Try to be very good at what we do.

10. Minimize waste and work that doesn't add value.

11. Allow the team to self-organize in order to obtain the best results.

12. Reflect on our successes and failures.

Chapter 6: Wasting time is a crime

6.1 Invest time only in productive tasks

The time we dedicate to our Business has to add value. We call **waste** to **anything that consumes time and does not add value**. Waste makes us lose money and, therefore, we must avoid it at all costs.

I have already spoken of the principle of continuous improvement. Precisely for this reason it is so important, at regular intervals, to evaluate what we do to detect any daily activity that is wasteful.

For example, in the software industry of the 1960s, where the teams were not trusted nor the professionalism of the individual, the organizations protected themselves by creating complicated procedures that ensured an acceptable quality, even with "mediocre" teams. There was so much staff turnover in the teams (the employees were unhappy and they went to other companies), that everything had to be well tied, so huge amounts of time were spent generating thousands of pages of documentation. Documentation that was impossible to read and that was never updated. That is a good example of waste. Generating that amount of documentation did not add value and was a way to waste time and money. And all because there was no faith in people and the opinion about the workers was terrible. This fact traumatized the creators of the Agile Manifesto, to such an extent that one of the values speaks explicitly of creating software that works instead of having exhaustive documentation.

Antonio Montes Orozco

If we remove that negative vision of the human race and trust the team members, we no longer need to protect ourselves in this way, so that the generation of so much documentation and the creation of "mediocre proof" procedures can be eliminated. If we eliminate waste, the time we dedicate is 100% effective in contributing value and we start earning money and with the same effort.

6.2 Avoid multitasking

Perform a very simple and quick test: measure the time it takes you to write the numbers from 1 to 20 in a row and numbers from 1 to 20, also in a row, but in Roman format (I, II, III, IV, V, VI, …)

Now repeat the same operation, but write the number 1 in decimal format and, right next to it, in Roman format, and so on with the rest of numbers, until 20.

FORM 1:

1 2 3 4 5 6 7 8 9 10 11 12 13 14 15 16 17 18 19 20

I II III IV V VI VII VIII IX X XI XII XIII XIV XV XVI XVII XVIII XIX XX

FORM 2:

1 I 2 II 3 III 4 IV 5 V 6 VI 7 VII 8 VIII 9 IX 10 X 11 XI 12 XII 13 XIII 14 XIV 15 XV 16 XVI 17 XVII 18 XVIII 19 XIX 20 XX

Antonio Montes Orozco

The test, if you have done it well, will show you that it takes more time with the second form than with the first one. The reason is because, in the second test, you have to change from thinking in decimal numeration to thinking in Roman numeration. You are multitasking. The switching time between tasks causes it to slow down and, therefore, takes longer in the second form.

Jeff Sutherland (inventor of Scrum) is very emphatic when he insists that the human being is not good in multitasking mode (Sutherland, 2014). We are educated in the belief that a person who performs multiple tasks at once is more efficient than someone who only performs one task at a time. This is a mistake: the result of multitasking is lower quality at work and greater exhaustion. When we change between tasks, we have to remember where we left off, what takes time, and get back into rhythm, which takes us even longer. In the end we are wasting time (and money). It would be much more productive to concentrate on one task, finish it, and then move on to the next one.

In addition, there is another reason: if you undertake a single task and finish it, when you deliver it, you are already receiving feedback on whether that is what the client wanted or not. If, on the other hand, you are at the same time with four tasks, in the end you will not finish any of them and you will not have received any feedback, apart from the fact that you will not have contributed anything of real value to your Business.

As I have already indicated, a delivered task adds value and gives rise to receive feedback from the client. A task left halfway is like having nothing, because it does not add value and we lose the opportunity to know if we are getting closer to our client's goal.

Therefore, multitasking is one more way to waste time: avoid it.

6.3 Summary

- Invest time only in productive tasks that add value to Business.

- Avoid multitasking. It is one more way to waste time because, when changing from one task to another, you have to remember where you were going, and you have to pick up the rhythm again.

- Remember, wasting time is a crime: it makes us lose money.

Chapter 7: Overview of Scrum

The word Scrum refers to the melee of rugby sport. The melee is when all the players embrace and join to decide the game tactics they will use. This already gives us an idea of the importance of teamwork in Scrum.

The Scrum framework consists of a series of roles, meetings (called **ceremonies**) and **artifacts** that form a vocabulary of their own and that is good to know. The rules prescribed by Scrum help create a high-performance team and contribute value iteratively and incrementally, as I explained above:

- **Iterative** means that the product or work is "cut up" and delivered in successive iterations. Each iteration is called **Sprint**.

- **Incremental** means that the product or work is not delivered completely. Each Sprint adds something more of value to what was delivered in the previous Sprint. That portion of work delivered is called **Increment**, and is one of the artifacts of Scrum.

If the work or product to be delivered were a car, in the first Sprint we would receive the chassis with the engine and wheels; in the following the body; in the following the seats; later the electrical installation, with the air conditioning included; and so on. With each delivery, the client sees if they like the design and if the product is adjusted to their expectations. Imagine that the client wanted the car red. Suppose that, in the Sprint where the body is shown, what is delivered is a white car. The client, when seeing it, realizes that they wanted the car red and that they didn't specify it. They notify the team and it takes note of the given feedback. With this methodology, the client will have at the end their stunning red car.

The steps that must be taken to start applying Scrum are:

1. Define who will assume each role:

> - Define who will be the team leader or **Scrum Master**.

> - Define who will be responsible for the product or work that needs to be done. This role is called the **Product Owner**. The Product Owner is the client's representative. Being a member of the team, it is like having the client within the team, collaborating side by side with everyone. Here it is observed that the traditional role of project manager unfolds in two roles: one that leads the team (Scrum Master role), and another that leads the work to be delivered (Product Owner role).

> - Define who will be the team members (**Development Team**). Although the word development has a clear connotation to software development, think about the team that carries out the work and develops it. The team consisting of Scrum Master, Product Owner and Development Team is called the **Scrum Team**.

> - Define who will be the rest of the **Stakeholders**: client, users, collaborators, etc.

2. Set the duration of each Sprint. In software development it is very easy to create deliveries that add value to Business. But, in other areas different from software development, this may not be so easy. Therefore, each type

of business must find a Sprint duration that is as small as possible, but that allows to contribute something of value in the delivery. It is usual for Sprints to last two weeks but, if at that time you see that you are not able to finish anything that adds value, extend the duration of the Sprint to what suits your Business.

3. Know what tasks need to be done. To do this, you have to divide the work or project into tasks that can be done in a Sprint. If a task does not fit in a Sprint, it will have to be cut up into smaller tasks that do fit. All tasks form the **Product Backlog**. The Product Owner is responsible for the Product Backlog being created and prioritized. By prioritizing we understand that the tasks that contribute more value will occupy the first positions of the list. Cutting the work up into tasks is an art, because they all have to add value to Business and they all have to fit in a Sprint.

4. Meet to plan the first Sprint. This is the **Sprint Planning** meeting. The tasks that the team can commit to have carried out the end of the Sprint are chosen, thus forming the **Sprint Backlog**.

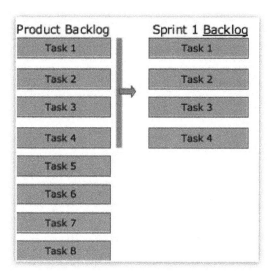

Figure 7.1 The Sprint Backlog is formed from the Product Backlog. The Product Backlog must be previously refined and prioritized. Author: Antonio Montes.

5. Once the Sprint has started, the team meets daily for all members to synchronize. This meeting is called **Daily Scrum,** or even simply "**Daily**".

6. Go refining the tasks of the Product Backlog that are candidates to enter the next Sprint, so that it is clear what needs to be done. These periodic meetings are called **Backlog Refinement**. In the Product Backlog the last tasks are not very refined and are mere declarations of intentions. As the Sprint that can undertake them approaches, they are refined and worked with the team, until they are completely defined. It is at this time that the tasks are said to be ready or that they meet the "**Definition of Ready**" or **DoR**, and it is another concept of the Scrum vocabulary.

7. After finishing the first Sprint, show the client what has been done, to receive the feedback of this. This meeting is known as **Sprint Review**. The product or work finished in a Sprint is called **Increment**. The tasks, to be considered finished, must meet the "**Definition of Done**" or **DoD** that has been agreed upon, another concept of Scrum to take into account.

8. Stop and reflect on how the Sprint march has gone, thus applying continuous improvement (*Kaizen*, do you remember?) And be more and more productive. This meeting is called **Sprint Retrospective**.

9. Repeat the cycle again, planning another Sprint, and so on constantly: do you remember the OODA? Constantly Observe, Orient, Decide and Act.

Summary

Scrum consists of a vocabulary of its own that you have to know. This vocabulary is formed by:

- 3 roles: Scrum Master, Product Owner and Development Team

- 5 meetings or ceremonies: Sprint Planning, Daily Scrum, Backlog Refinement, Sprint Review and Sprint Retrospective.

- 3 artifacts: Product Backlog, Sprint Backlog and Increment.

Once the new vocabulary is introduced, let's look at each role, ceremony and artifact in detail.

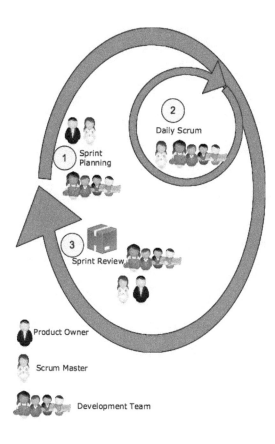

Figure 7.2 Scrum iterative cycle, where planning and reviewing are repeated in each Sprint, and synchronization meetings are repeated daily (Daily Scrum). Author: Antonio Montes.

Antonio Montes Orozco

Chapter 8: Roles in Scrum

8.1 Scrum Master

The Scrum Master is the facilitator leader of Ouchi's Theory Z (to give confidence to the team and understand that everyone is looking for self-actualization and is willing to take on responsibilities and being trusted, do you remember?). They are not a boss, but a leader. Therefore, they do not assign the work and do not say how things are done, but they facilitate the team's work, providing what it needs to do its work and eliminating impediments.

They are both mentor and coach. Mentor means teaching the team the Scrum methodology and the principles of Agilism. Coach means getting the most out of the team, knowing how to ask the right questions. A coach is not a counselor, but someone who listens attentively and helps you reflect on the right questions, so that you are the one who reaches the conclusions by yourself. Coaching is an art.

It is also responsible for monitoring the state of the team, detecting possible dysfunctions (do you remember the five dysfunctions of Lencioni?). If a team member feels uneasy or upset, the Scrum Master will have a private session with this person and, through coaching techniques, will listen to their problems and help them find the answers they are looking for. Coaching techniques have nothing to do with manipulating, but with listening carefully, connecting with the person and building together from there. A typical coaching question is "how are you going to do this?" In this way the coach helps the "coachee" to find the answers. Many times, the answer to the problems is in ourselves, only that we do not know how to ask the right questions. Saying that "something is impossible" does not contribute anything, but asking "how am I going to achieve this?" is a very powerful question that puts our brain to work to find a solution.

Another mission of the Scrum Master is to manage to get the team self-organized, without the need for this role anymore. It can be paradoxical, and it should be one of the few jobs where its purpose is to be made dispensed with. It may sound self-destructive, but it is what it should be. That is why I always say that the work of Scrum Master is vocational: it is the team that takes the credit for successes and there is never recognition for this role. The Scrum Master is in the shade, supporting the team and facilitating its work. A self-organized team meets without being proposed by the Scrum Master and resolves the impediments on its own.

Nowadays, the work of the Scrum Master is not understood in the companies and I can still find job offers where knowledge that is typical of a software developer is requested for the role of Scrum Master. It's better that they are not technical experts, so as not to "rule the team". The less they know about the work the team does, the less they will act as a "counselor", and the more they will act as a coach.

Antonio Montes Orozco

8.2 Product Owner

The Product Owner is responsible for ensuring that the Product Backlog is updated and prioritized. They are the Business representative within the team and their figure reflects the close collaboration between Business and the Development Team.

Their function is to negotiate with users and clients and to be constantly analyzing the Product Backlog, so that it is updated and prioritized.

A Product Owner must understand that the team works by pulling, and not by pushing. The team pulls the tasks from the Sprint Backlog. Their role has nothing to do with the classic figure of a project manager. They do not assign the tasks, but the team pulls them from the Sprint Backlog (that is precisely what it means that the team works by pulling on demand).

If the Product Owner does their job well, the Product Backlog will contain tasks that are well prioritized and ready to be undertaken by the team. The team will move forward at a constant and sustainable pace and will move forward tasks with Business value. As this list is prioritized, the tasks that the team is going ahead with are those that produce the most return on investment. A Product Owner who does not do their job leaves the team out in the cold, especially at the Sprint Planning meeting, because the team does not know what tasks to undertake.

It is the responsibility of the Product Owner to refine the Product Backlog regularly, so that the candidate tasks to enter the next Sprint are prepared to be undertaken by the team, and comply with the DoR (Definition of Ready).

Antonio Montes Orozco

8.3 Development Team

The Development Team is self-organized and empowered, that is, they are given the confidence to decide how they will perform the tasks. The Product Owner decides what, but the Development Team decides how. Precisely for being involved and deciding how, it commits itself (remember Stephen Covey and his principle that there is no commitment without involvement). A truly self-organized team works alone and does not need the figure of the Scrum Master to meet daily in the Daily Scrum. But that is not easily achieved and they may need the Scrum Master for weeks or even indefinitely.

The Development Teams, apart from being self-organized, are multidisciplinary. This means that they are able to do the job as a whole. For example, if we are with projects of remodeling houses, the Development Team will contain a plasterer, an electrician, a plumber, etc. Its size should be between 3 and 7 members. If smaller, it could not bring the works to completion, and if larger, it could imply a communication problem in the team.

The fact that a team is not multidisciplinary and cannot undertake the work by itself implies dependencies with other specialists or with other departments, if we are talking about a large organization. Having external dependencies brings nothing but problems, because the areas or the specialists on whom they depend may not apply Scrum, or they may not be adapted to the rhythm of delivery by Sprints. This circumstance may prevent Scrum from being applied.

Antonio Montes Orozco

Chapter 9: Meetings or ceremonies in Scrum

Scrum establishes a series of meetings, in which the context is created so that the team involves in the decisions and can commit itself.

9.1 Sprint Planning

This meeting takes place before the Sprint begins. In it, the Product Owner presents the tasks stated in the Product Backlog. The team estimates task by task. Notice that trust is given to the team so that it is the one that estimates the effort that will entail doing the work. It is the empowerment or trust that we saw in Theory Z. Since it is the team the one that is going to carry out the work, it is only up to it to estimate the effort that will be involved. The Scrum Master facilitates the meeting, but does not estimate. The Product Owner is there to answer questions, but they do not estimate either. This meeting cannot be reached with unrefined tasks, because a lot of time would be wasted trying to find out what needs to be done, what implications the job has or what dependencies there are. Therefore, before arriving at this meeting, you need to have several Refinement meetings of the Product Backlog. It is the responsibility of the Product Owner that this occurs.

When the team has estimated several tasks and believes that it has already reached the maximum of these that can be undertaken in a Sprint, stops estimating and build the Sprint Backlog, which will contain all those tasks that have been selected to be performed in the Sprint about to start.

Antonio Montes Orozco

It is highly recommended that the Sprint tasks are written on sticky notes that are then sticked on a panel (or a wall, or a window or wherever). The human being prefers visuals and, as we will see later, it is better that the whole team can meet around the visual panel with the tasks of the Sprint. Scrum prescribes the duration of this meeting, but it is better to find out what is the right duration for your team.

It is a key meeting, because it is where the commitment of the team is forged before the work that is coming. It is a long meeting that can take more than a couple of hours, so keep that in mind.

9.2 Daily Scrum or *"Daily"*

Daily the team meets so that all the members can synchronize with each other. In it, each member of the team answers the following three questions:

1. What did I do yesterday?

2. What impediment did I encounter on my way?

3. What am I going to do today?

This meeting is quick, about fifteen minutes, so as not to waste time. It is important that it is always done at the same time and in the same place. To emphasize the brevity of this meeting, it is usually done standing up, so that the members of the team do not get too comfortable.

A typical failure happens when Development Team members address the Scrum Master to give them the progress report. That is a mistake, because the Scrum Master is the leader, but they are not the "boss". Each member of the team, when speaking, has to address the rest of their teammates, as it is a synchronization meeting between all of them. The impediments that are announced will be resolved by the team, and the Scrum Master will help solve them.

The Product Owner does not usually intervene, except to answer questions. They do not have to attend the meeting. Let us remember that the Product Owner is not the "boss" either. In this methodology there are no bosses: there are roles and a lot of teamwork.

This is the favorite meeting of the teams and they see its value from the beginning. The public exhibition of what we have done and the problems we have encountered implies the implementation of full involvement. At the same time, it reaffirms our commitment to the tasks to be carried out, helping us to be more focused on the daily work, since we will have to give an account of it in the "*Daily*" of the next day.

9.3 Backlog Refinement

In the Product Backlog, the tasks occupying the lowest positions are the lowest priority. They are often just mere intentions that the Product Owner has, regarding the work that needs to be done. As the Sprint that may undertake these tasks is approaching, these must be refined so that the team understands them and dissipates any doubt that may have regarding their resolution: dependencies, foreseeable difficulties, associated risks, etc. The refined tasks are ready to be undertaken by the Development Team and they go on to comply with the **DoR** (Definition of Ready).

Antonio Montes Orozco

Therefore, the Product Owner will convene the team, at regular intervals, to refine the Product Backlog.

A quality Product Backlog is one where the first tasks, with the highest priority, are all refined (comply with the DoR) and ready to be undertaken by the Development Team. As we move away from the first positions, the tasks will be less refined.

9.4 Sprint Review

In this meeting the team shows the Product Owner what it has achieved during the Sprint that has just finished. The Product Owner gives feedback on what is presented and clarifies ideas. In this way, the Development Team has a very valuable feedback on what is being delivered and can adjust its effort in the desired direction by the Product Owner. It also serves for the Product Owners to clarify ideas about what they really want. It is the case that many times the client does not know what they want until they are shown something and then they can clarify their ideas.

This iterative process is done in each Sprint and is the result of the OODA process (Observe, Orient, Decide and Act) that Jeff Sutherland learned in the Air Force.

9.5 Sprint Retrospective

This is one of the most important meetings in Scrum, because it is where the team learns from mistakes and matures (*Kaizen* or continuous improvement, remember?). It is a meeting to reflect on what practices have been successful and must be maintained, and what practices can be improved. At the meeting, the team debates openly and with confidence, committing to concrete actions for improvement. This meeting takes place at the end of the Sprint and after having had the Sprint Review.

The duration of this meeting can be several hours, so keep it in mind for the first one you organize.

Throughout my professional life I have met people who did not see value in this meeting. These people belonged both to the management of the company and to the middle management staff, or even to the members of the Development Team. Continuous improvement or *Kaizen* is what allows a team to learn from mistakes and to be increasingly efficient, until forming a high-performance team, which will carry out twice the work in half the time. It is a process of months, but it is worth persevering and having faith. If the improvement actions are not followed up, the team may stop seeing the value of this meeting. For this reason, I advise you to follow up on the actions that are decided to take and, at the beginning of this meeting, make a review of how is the status of the actions that were decided in the previous Sprint Retrospective.

9.6 Summary

In this chapter we have looked closely at the meetings or ceremonies which Scrum consists of:

- Sprint Planning, which would be the first one and is where the team commits to what it will do in the next Sprint that is about to start.

- Daily Scrum (or *"Daily"*), which is the daily synchronization meeting that the team performs.

- Backlog Refinement. It is a meeting requested by the Product Owner to leave the following tasks that will enter the next Sprint prepared. The result of the refinement must be compliance with the DoR (Definition of Ready) for the following tasks that are in the Product Backlog.

- Sprint Review. After finishing a Sprint, the Product Owner is shown the result, to receive Business feedback and readjust.

- Sprint Retrospective. The team reflects on what needs to be maintained, because it is going well, and what needs to be improved. This reflection is what creates high-performance teams.

Chapter 10: Artifacts in Scrum

10.1 Product Backlog

The Product Backlog is the list of all the tasks that must be done to finish the job. They are prioritized based on the value they bring to the Business, so the first ones are those that provide more value and the last ones those providing less.

It is the responsibility of the Product Owner to prioritize them and carry out periodic refinement sessions with the team. The tasks that are candidates to enter the next Sprint must be ready to be undertaken by the team (that meet the DoR or "definition of ready", do you remember?), hence it is so important to refine the eligible tasks of being undertaken in the next Sprint.

If we know the Velocity of the team and estimate the remaining tasks to be done of the Product Backlog, we can have an estimate of the Sprints we would need to finish all the work.

Let us remember that it is the responsibility of the Product Owner to keep the Product Backlog up to date.

We have commented that the tasks have to be prioritized based on the value they bring to the Business, but there are tasks that are very quick to do and provide little value, so it may be worth prioritizing them against others that provide more value but they are longer to finish. Therefore, to prioritize, tasks can be placed in a cost-value matrix. Those that cost little to do and provide great value would be candidates to enter the first. Then come those that cost a lot to do and do not provide much value.

10.2 Sprint Backlog

The Sprint Backlog is the list of tasks that will be undertaken in the Sprint that is about to start. They are prioritized based on the value they bring to Business. In chapter 11 I will explain how it is estimated and, in chapter 12, I will explain what the team's Velocity is, and how it is used to know to what task the team can commit, facing the next Sprint. We will also see, in Chapter 11, what the story points are and how they are used in the estimates. After the Sprint Planning meeting, it is the responsibility of the Scrum Master to create the Sprint Backlog and present it to the Product Owner to be informed.

During the Sprint, the Sprint Backlog cannot be modified, as it is a closed commitment between the Product Owner and the team. Like everything in life, there may be exceptions, but always agreed upon and negotiated with the Product Owner. But they must be exceptions. If, on a regular basis, the Sprint Backlog is broken and new tasks that are very urgent come in, Scrum may not suit your Business and you may have to explore other agile methodologies, such as Kanban, for example.

10.3 Increment

The Increment is the part of the job that finishes at the end of the Sprint. The part finished adds value to the Business. As the Product Owner has been careful to prioritize the tasks, that Increment is what could bring more value to the client. There are still tasks to be done, but they are not so important nor provide so much value. The Increment is not all that needs to be done, but it is the most important thing. Therefore the client, seeing it, can already get an idea of what is going to be delivered at the end, and can already give valuable feedback at the Sprint Review meeting.

We must try that what is delivered can already be used by the client. If the job is to make financial reports, the Increment would be to have some report ready to be delivered to the client. If the work is for renovations in a house, the Increment would be to have a part ready for the client to settle and enjoy it. Or, if the work consists of the students of a school learning a subject, the Increment would consist of having already studied one of the lessons of the syllabus.

10.4 Minimum Viable Product (MVP)

Although the MVP is not an official Scrum artifact, it is a widespread concept in the universe of Agilism. It is about determining what is the minimum that can be done, that can be delivered to the client and that provides value. For example, if we have to generate a group of ten economic reports, the MVP would consist of having at least the two or three main reports that contribute more value. By delivering the MVP to the client, they would already have the most valuable reports and could give the team a feedback on what they have found.

10.5 Summary

In chapter 7, when I introduced the Scrum vocabulary, I told you about artifacts. In this chapter we have seen them more extensively: Product Backlog, Sprint Backlog and Increment.

The Product Backlog includes all the tasks that must be performed, prioritized based on the value they bring to the Business. In the prioritization it is also good to take into account the effort that will entail carrying them out.

The Sprint Backlog contains the tasks that the team commits to finishing in a Sprint. We have seen that the Sprint Backlog is a commitment of the team and that it is not good to modify it during the Sprint. If it is often done, it would be more interesting to use Kanban, for example.

The Increment is the set of tasks finished in a Sprint. These are tasks that add value to the Business and that, therefore, the customer can use already, thus giving valuable feedback to the team.

Finally I have presented the concept of MVP (Minimum Viable Product), which is a term widely used in the world of Agilism. It is the minimum portion of product that we can put in the hands of the client and that provides value.

Antonio Montes Orozco

Chapter 11: Estimating tasks

We have seen that, in the Sprint Planning meeting, the team estimates the effort involved in each task, in order to know which tasks of the Product Backlog can be compromised in the next Sprint, but, how are the tasks estimated? What mechanism is used?

11.1 The human being is better at comparing than estimating times

The human being is an expert at comparing things with each other. For example, if we know the height of a building and we take it as a reference, we can estimate the height of the surrounding buildings. If the height of the building at hand is X, by comparison, we can deduce that the height of the adjacent buildings is 2X and 3X, respectively. It costs us nothing to estimate by comparison, taking as reference what we know.

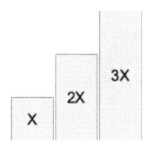

Figure 11.1 Estimation by comparison with a known reference. Known the height of a building (X), we calculate the height of the adjacent buildings by comparison.

Antonio Montes Orozco

However, the human being is not good at estimating based on time. We tend to go above or below. In classic project management two errors have traditionally been committed:

- The first one, estimating based on time. In the past, the team was not empowered and trusted, so the team had to face impossible delivery dates. This meant that, on the rare occasions when they were consulted, they gave very comfortable times in the estimates, to avoid overtime and stressful working rhythms.

- The second error, not taking into account the team for the estimates. As you have learned, this leads to the team not being able to commit to the estimate that the project manager has made for them, because without involvement there is no commitment (Stephen Covey principle, do you remember?).

So, if it is not good to estimate based on time, what unit do we use as a reference to estimate? In the next section I will present the concept of *story point*.

11.2 The concept of story point

In Scrum, tasks (also called *user stories*) are estimated based on story points. A story point is the effort involved in making the simplest possible task. For example, if we are a remodeling company, we can agree that the simplest task we can undertake is to install a plug. We associate a story point and the rest of tasks are estimated by comparison with it. If, for example, putting a tile is twice as complicated as putting a plug, we estimate it in two story points.

In order to estimate, we have infinite possibilities. To limit the possible values, the Fibonacci series are used. We see it below.

11.3 The Fibonacci series

The Fibonacci series are of the form 0, 1, 2, 3, 5, 8, 13, 21, 34, etc. If you notice, each number is the sum of the two previous numbers. Therefore, we can only choose 1 story point, or 2, or 3, or 5, etc. That simplifies our estimation. In addition, the use of Fibonacci series has another great property, which is to compensate complexity. Let's imagine that we are evaluating the complexity of removing a window and changing it. We cannot choose 25 or 30, so we choose 34, which is the value closest to what we are thinking. The Fibonacci series, as they increase more and more, compensate for the estimation given to more complex tasks.

To avoid having to note down the Fibonacci series every time we estimate at a Sprint Planning meeting, the Scrum estimate cards were invented (also called **Scrum Planning Poker Cards)**. I was very surprised the first time I saw them. More surprised I stayed when I found out that there were even applications for smartphones.

11.4 Planning Poker Cards and their use in the estimation

Remember when I explained the Sprint Planning meeting. In this meeting the tasks that were going to enter in the next Sprint were estimated. The process to estimate each task is the following one:

1. The Product Owner explains the task, which has already been refined previously.

2. The members of the team discuss the complexity of the task, its repercussions and possible dependencies.

3. Team members vote on the story points they are going to assign, choosing a card with the estimated value, but without showing it.

4. All at once show the cards. It is important that all of them do so at the same time, to prevent team leaders from influencing the voting of their peers.

5. Some will agree, but others will have estimated more points and others less. A dialogue is established, where the most optimistic and the most pessimistic explain their reasons.

6. The voting process is repeated until all are aligned and reach a consensus.

With practice this process is done very quickly. Since the cards only contain the values of the Fibonacci series, there is not much to choose from. This accelerates the estimation process. This way of estimating, where everyone knows the value chosen by the rest, is called **Wideband Delphi**. It is a method created in the 70s and is widely used in the agile world.

It is empirically demonstrated that the resulting estimate is very close to the real effort involved in the task. Scrum has been around for many years and is the most extended agile framework. There are years of practice behind its back, with proven results. Believe me, this way of estimating is very precise, although it may not seem so. It is hard to work at the beginning with a concept as abstract as the story point, but then the team gets used to it and the accuracy and predictability become amazing.

11.5 Ideal days

Another practice is to assimilate a story point to an ideal day. That is, a story point would be the work that can be done in a workday, where the worker is not interrupted and is fully dedicated to the task. Hence, it is called ideal day.

To use ideal days is perverse, since the abstract concept of the story point is changed by the temporal dimension. Let's recall that the human being is not good at estimating based on time, so accuracy will be lost in the estimates.

In the next chapter we will see how all these concepts are related to the team's Velocity.

11.6 Summary

- We have seen that the human being does not estimate well based on time. In fact, it is one of the reasons why classic projects do not usually end on time.

- If we take the simplest task as a reference, the rest can be estimated based on the reference task, by comparison. Oddly, the human being is an expert at making comparisons.

- The basic measure is the story point, which is equivalent to the effort of performing the simplest task.

- To choose the possible values, the Fibonacci series are used. This gives us two advantages: it reduces the number of possible values, and the high values compensate us for the estimation of the most complex tasks.

- Another practice is to use ideal days. A story point would be the work that can be done in an ideal working day, without interruptions, but I do not advise using them. Later, when I will explain the concept of Velocity, it will be clear why it is not convenient to use ideal days.

- There are estimation cards, called Scrum Planning Poker Cards. There are even applications of Scrum Planning Poker Cards for the smartphone.

Antonio Montes Orozco

Chapter 12: Velocity

12.1 Definition of Velocity

The Velocity in Scrum is defined as the amount of story points that the team is able to finish in each Sprint. In the first Sprint we don't know the real Velocity of the team, apart from the fact that the team is probably not used to working together and is not high-performance. But, in the first Sprint, a series of story points will be taken forward, so we'll have an approximation of the Velocity that the team starts to have. The Velocity will also indicate to us, in the Sprint Planning meeting, the amount of tasks to which we can commit ourselves. Thus, Sprint to Sprint, we will readjust and know our real Velocity, so we will start to be "predictable".

12.2 Team's predictability

A team is predictable when it complies with the story points which it commits itself with. Therefore, it is vital that the team knows its Velocity. A team that knows its Velocity is committed, in the planning of the next Sprint, to finish the story points that knows that it can take ahead, being thus tremendously predictable.

If the team estimates the tasks of the Product Backlog, you can have a very accurate estimate of the remaining Sprints to finish all the work that needs to be done. This is very important to know if everything can be delivered, or if it will be necessary to remove less important functionality to be able to reach a delivery date, in case there is one.

12.3 Commitment to Sprint Planning

For example, let's consider a team where there are 6 tasks in the Product Backlog. We know that the team has a Velocity of 45 story points per Sprint. At the planning meeting, the team estimates and assigns each task the following estimates:

- Task 1 = 13 story points

- Task 2 = 20 story points

- Task 3 = 8 story points

- Task 4 = 2 story points

- Task 5 = 20 story points

- Task 6 = 2 story points

Looking to commit to the next Sprint, the team is choosing tasks in order, because they are prioritized, and the first are those that provide more value. Adding story points, we see that up to task 4 we have 43 story points, so task 5 would not fit, which is 20 story points, and the team's Velocity is 45 story points. Therefore, the task 5 is left out, entering in its place the task 6, that only implies 2 story points, adding therefore the 45 story points that marks the team's Velocity.

Antonio Montes Orozco

The whole team has estimated and the whole team has participated in the planning, so the whole team is committed to take out tasks 1, 2, 3, 4, and 6 in the next Sprint.

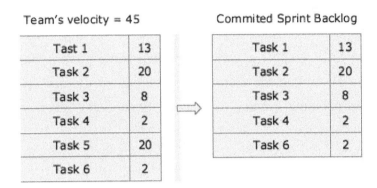

Team's velocity = 45

Tast 1	13
Task 2	20
Task 3	8
Task 4	2
Task 5	20
Task 6	2

Commited Sprint Backlog

Task 1	13
Task 2	20
Task 3	8
Task 4	2
Task 6	2

Figure 12.1 Example of how the Sprint Backlog is constructed from the Product Backlog, based on the team's Velocity and the estimates of the tasks.

12.4 Evolution of Velocity

The Velocity should increase and the team should be able to finish more and more story points in each Sprint. But this rule does not have to be fulfilled if, instead of using story points, ideal days are used in the estimates. Let's imagine that we have a Development Team of 5 professionals. In two weeks, 50 ideal working days could be completed (10 ideal days per person, 5 ideal days per person and week). That is the job they could take forward and it will always be the same, so their Velocity will remain constant over time. In addition, ideal days introduce the variable time, with all the perversion that entails (bad estimates and the feeling that the Velocity is stagnant).

However, a team that uses story points and abstracts from the dimension of time will see how its Velocity gradually grows and how it estimates increasingly better, being more and more productive.

12.5 Summary

- In this chapter we present the concept of team's Velocity, which is defined as the number of story points that the team finishes by Sprint.

- Knowing the Velocity allows the team to be predictable and to know how many Sprints are left to finish all the work.

- The Velocity is not known in Sprint 1 but, Sprint to Sprint, it is discovered and allows to be predictable. Being predictable means that the team really ends the story points committed in the Sprint Planning meeting.

- Velocity is a parameter that should increase over time, unless ideal days are used in the estimation. With story points it is observed how the team is more and more productive, while, with ideal days, the committed points will always be the same. Therefore, I recommend abstracting from the dimension of time and using story points instead.

Antonio Montes Orozco

Chapter 13: What to do with stories that cannot be finished during the Sprint

We have learned how to estimate the effort that user stories (tasks, do you remember?) will entail. We have learned the concept of story point to estimate and how it is applied to calculate the productivity or team's Velocity. As always, the theory is clear and it seems easy to apply it but, when you come down to reality, you realize that things are not so simple and that there are many exceptions to the rule that you have to know how to manage. One of them has to do with what is done when, at the end of a Sprint, time has not been given to complete all the stories committed. The strict point of view tells us that, if it is not finished, it seems as if nothing has been delivered, thus impacting the Velocity of the team. This fact is very disappointing to the teams, because they have been working and have completed story points, only that they haven't finished any user story that has been left halfway. It is then when the perverse practices begin to mask the Velocity, where all the work done is reflected.

If the teams are determined to mask their Velocity, we should ask ourselves if they feel watched and if they are losing confidence. When a team feels watched and feels that its economic benefit (whether in the form of a bonus or any other economic incentive) depends on the Velocity-based metric, we can be sure that it will become obsessed with the fact that everything that has been done "counts".

Antonio Montes Orozco

Therefore, I will discuss some practices that I have seen throughout my professional life, clarifying which ones seem reasonable to me and which ones I advise against.

13.1 Strategy 1: Accumulate the story points for the next Sprint

Be an estimated user story in 10 story points. At the end of Sprint 1 the story is not finished. The team estimates that, out of the 10 initial story points, about 7 have been made but, since the story has not been completed, the delivered points are 0, and it counts 0 points for the Velocity. For the next Sprint (Sprint 2), the same story enters again, being estimated again at 10 story points. As there are only 3 points left to finish, the story is finished in Sprint 2, so it is considered that 10 story points have been delivered, when, in reality, only 3 story points have been made. Therefore, accumulate the story points for the next Sprint is to assign to the user story, for the next Sprint, the initial story points that were estimated. I consider this practice correct and the team is free to choose it.

13.2 Strategy 2: Re-estimate the user story for the next Sprint

Be an estimated user story in 10 story points. At the end of Sprint 1 the story is not finished. The team estimates that, out of the 10 initial story points, about 7 have been made but, since the story has not been completed, the points delivered are 0, and it counts 0 points for the Velocity. For the next Sprint (Sprint 2), the same story re-enters again, estimated at 3 story points, which are those remaining to be completed. As the story was almost finished, at the end of the Sprint it is possible to finish it, so 3 story points have been considered to be delivered. Therefore, re-estimating consists of assigning to the user story, for the next Sprint, the story points that are considered to be left. I consider this practice correct and the team is free to choose it.

13.3 Strategy 3: Re-estimate the story in the middle of the Sprint to finish it

Be an estimated user story in 10 story points. The end of Sprint 1 is approaching and the story has not yet been finalized, estimating that, out of the 10 initial points, only 7 have been made. The team is obsessed with fulfilling its commitment so, in the middle of the Sprint, it re-estimates the story in 7 points, to be able to deliver 7 points at the end of the Sprint and give the feeling that they have delivered the commitment. This is a way of masking the stories that are not completed and denotes that there is no confidence in the team to be transparent, which can be a symptom of fear of not fulfilling the commitment. Therefore, re-estimating the user story in the middle of the Sprint is to assign to the story the story points that are known to be over, thus giving a false sense of commitment delivery. The objective is to be truly predictable and to know how to divide the work into stories that fit in a Sprint, managing the dependencies with time. If the user stories are re-estimated in the middle of the Sprint, there is a danger of generating distrust in the Product Owner and in the team itself. Therefore, **this practice is discouraged**.

13.4 Summary

The user stories that are not finished at the end of the Sprint, contribute 0 story points to the Velocity. It is as if nothing has been done, even if something has been worked on. Being strict requires a better partition work into user stories and that they are better refined, to resolve dependencies, risks or doubts that may exist. Even so, teams that feel watched and pressured can perform various practices so that the work done "counts" in the Velocity. In the following table I show a summary of the three strategies that we have just seen.

Sprint 1	Sprint 2	Strategy
Estimated = 10 Delivered = 0 Finished = 7	Estimated = 10 Delivered = 10 Finished = 3	Accumulate story points for the next Sprint. I think it's correct.
Estimated = 10 Delivered = 0 Finished = 7	Estimated = 3 Delivered = 3 Finished = 3	Re-estimate in the next Sprint. I think it's correct.
Estimated = 10 Re-estimated = 7 Delivered = 7 Finished = 7	Estimated = 3 Delivered = 3 Finished = 3	Re-estimate in the middle of the Sprint so that what is done coincides with the estimate. I advise against it.

Chapter 14: Visual panels (Kanban)

You may have read something about Scrum and have seen that sticky notes are sticked on foam core boards or portable whiteboards. Effectively, they are used. Why? Because the human being is tremendously visual and assimilates tasks better when they are written on a sticky note than when the tasks are in a spreadsheet or in a digital tool (such as JIRA, Trello, LeanKit, etc.). Similarly, physically updating the status of a task, moving it from a column to another one on a panel, is more in line with our way of being than connecting to a shared spreadsheet and updating the status of the task there.

In Scrum, **Kanban** panels are usually used for tasks. The word Kanban is a Japanese word meaning "**card**". Kanban panels are usually divided into columns, showing the tasks that are to be done, the tasks that are in process, the pending tasks to be verified and the tasks completed. But each team has to choose the columns that best suit them.

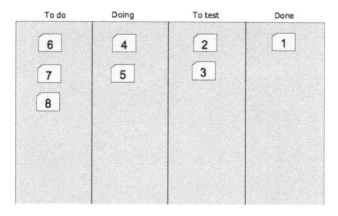

Figure 14.1 Kanban Panel with the task flow, where you can see which are to be done, which are in process, which are ready to verify, and which have already been completed. Author: Antonio Montes.

An advantage of Kanban panels is that they speak for themselves. Let's imagine that we have a team of 3 people and the panel reflects the information in Figure 14.2. Looking at the panel, we observe that there are 6 tasks that are being carried out at the same time, which suggests that the team is doing multitasking. We already saw how damaging it can be to change from one task to another. We also observed that the tasks are being accumulated in the test column (To test), which indicates that we have a bottleneck in the team.

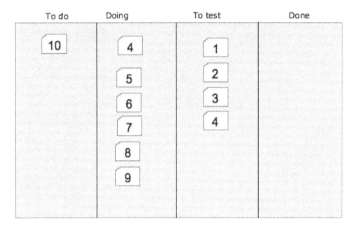

Figure 14.2 Kanban Panel with tasks, where it is appreciated that the team is multitasking and that there is a bottleneck in the test phase. Author: Antonio Montes.

We see that, at a glance, we have detected a bottleneck (the one in the verification column) and a bad practice within the team (that of multitasking). That is why Scrum places so much emphasis on using information as visually as possible.

Kanban panels fall into what are called **information radiators**. Scrum tends to make all information transparent and accessible. There is nothing to hide. If a manager wants to know how the status of the project is going, it is enough to go through the Kanban panel to see which tasks are in process, which are pending and which are already finished.

14.1 WIP

Already placed with Kanban panels, I will take advantage of introducing the concept of WIP, which is the **Work In Progress**. We should try to have the WIP as low as possible, to avoid multitasking (Do you remember the exercise of decimal numbers and Roman numerals in Chapter 6?). Limiting the WIP will make the team work more efficiently and be more productive. Limiting the WIP means that the team does not take on one more task until a member has been released so that they can undertake more work without falling into multitasking.

I understand that there are times when we get stuck with a task and we cannot continue, so it would be unproductive not to put on another task that is waiting in the Sprint Backlog. Therefore, the WIP can be limited to twice the number of team members, for example. In this way we would allow a maximum of two tasks at a time for each member of the team. Depending on the nature of your Business, you should find the right WIP for your case. But remember that it is best to keep it always as low as possible, to avoid the perverse effect of multitasking.

14.2 Summary

- In chapter 9, when we looked in detail at the Scrum ceremonies, I commented that the Daily was facing a panel with the tasks on sticky notes. In this chapter we have seen how a Kanban panel would be made and the meaning of this strange word ("card" in Japanese).

- Kanban panels speak for themselves and help us find bottlenecks or detect bad practices, such as multitasking.

- I've presented the concept of **WIP** as **Work In Progress**. The WIP must be minimized so that there is no multitasking and the team is more productive.

Chapter 15: How to start using Scrum

So far we have seen the principles and values which Scrum is based on. We have learned its own vocabulary, with its roles, ceremonies and artifacts. We have also seen how tasks (user stories) are estimated, the concept of Velocity and its relation to the predictability of the team. We have even seen what is that of Kanban panels and how a panel that is an information radiator is mounted.

Now we can see, with a practical example, how to implement Scrum in an environment that has nothing to do with the software. Remember that the key to Scrum is that it enhances teamwork and achieves commitment for everyone through involvement, so it is valid for any work that has to be done and that involves the synchronization of a team. For this, I propose to put ourselves in the place of a remodeling company that wants to use Scrum.

15.1 Example: Remodeling Company

I especially like this example, because Jeff Sutherland tells in his book, (Sutherland, 2014), that he wanted to make a remodeling in his apartment and he found out about a remodeling company that was famous in his neighborhood. They gave very accurate estimates and always delivered on time. When Jeff asked them how they did it, they told him that they had read a book that dealt with Scrum and that they put it into practice. Every day they made a Daily Scrum to synchronize. If the next task was to paint a room, for example, they agreed that they had to help remove the furniture, so all those who were free would help. Imagine that the electrician had no job for that day, so he would help remove furniture. This simple fact of synchronizing each day made them much more productive and that the work went according to the estimate made. Imagine Jeff's surprise when he discovered that his book, oriented to the world of software development, had transcended to be applied in other environments that he had never imagined.

Let's be a remodeling company and a project that consists of the remodeling of a living room, where the client wants to place a stereo music chain, for which he needs to protect it with a ground connection. The ground connection is not installed, so it will have to be taken, through grooves, to the plugs where the music chain will be connected. By the way, the floors will be fixed and the walls will be painted.

The first thing we need is to name the different roles.

15.2 Assignment of roles

We name the Product Owner, who will be the person in charge of dealing with the client and of obtaining their requirements. We'll then name the Scrum Master, who will be the team leader. We'll name the Development Team, which will be formed by the necessary specialists to undertake the remodeling: an electrician, a hardwood flooring installer, a painter and a mason.

It can be quite expensive to assign a Product Owner and a Scrum Master to the remodeling team, so in this case, it will be the team members who will adopt one of these roles. For example, the one who usually deals more with clients may be the one who acts as the Product Owner. The one who doesn't have a lot of work, like the electrician, can act as the Scrum Master, for example.

The Product Owner gets down to work, building a Product Backlog.

15.3 Creating the Product Backlog and the MPV

The Product Backlog could contain the following tasks:

1. Take the ground connection to the corner that the client has chosen.

2. Put new parquet in the living room.

3. Paint the walls of the living room.

The three tasks provide value for themselves, but the most valuable task is to take the ground to the corner that the client has chosen. With this task, the client will have what was proposed, which is to be able to listen to music with his new sound chain. Therefore, it is the first task of the Product Backlog.

The MPV would be made up of tasks 1 and 3, because, with these tasks, the client could listen to music in his living room and would not have to see a groove through his walls, since the walls would be already painted. You can leave for later the arrangement of the ground, because the main objective would already be achieved.

Antonio Montes Orozco

15.4 Creating the Sprint Backlog 1 in the Sprint Planning

It is the first meeting that takes place. In it, the remodeling team takes as reference the installation of a plug, which is assigned a story point. The remaining tasks are estimated by comparison with this:

1. Take the ground connection to the corner that the client has chosen: 8 story points.

2. Put new parquet in the room: 34 story points.

3. Paint the walls of the room: 21 story points.

I am not an expert in remodeling. The important thing in this exercise is not that the estimates are correct, but that you look at how to proceed to start applying Scrum. Now that we have a Product Backlog with estimated tasks, the team has to decide the duration of the Sprints and how many tasks are going to go into the first one. Due to the characteristic of the Business, the team reaches the agreement that the Sprints have to be one week, because it is enough time to deliver something that adds value to the client.

For the first Sprint, and based on their experience, the team commits to tasks 1 and 3. They do not believe they can undertake more than 30 history points. Tasks 1 and 3 add up to 29 story points between the two. It is a first approximation and thus the team will discover the Velocity that it has. Therefore, the team is committed to making the groove through which the grounding will go and painting the walls of the room, leaving the floor for the next Sprint. Therefore, they can have the MPV ready in the first Sprint, which will allow them to deliver something that adds value to the client.

15.5 Sprint 1

Sprint 1 starts and the team has its first Daily. The mason will start with the groove so that the electrician can install the ground wire through it. The electrician already knows, thanks to the Daily, that he will take action as soon as the mason has finished. To paint the walls of the room, what will be done as soon as the plaster is covering the groove and it has dried, they will have to clear furniture and go covering them so they do not get dirty with the paint. The hardwood flooring installer, the painter and the electrician get down to work to advance work. They will also cover the baseboards, the window frames and everything that is likely to be stained with paint.

In the second daily the mason communicates that he has finished making the groove to get the ground connection, so the electrician can already do his job. The living room is already with the furniture removed and covered, and the rest of the team has covered the baseboards and the window frames. The painter announces an impediment: it is necessary to agree with the client what color he wants the walls. The Scrum Master notifies the Product Owner, who contacts the client and both agree to put a sample on one of the walls. Another impediment has to do with the paintings, as the work progresses fast. The Scrum Master buys the paint that same day, along with the dye to make the samples agreed with the client.

Antonio Montes Orozco

In the third Daily it becomes clear that the state of work is as follows: the groove to install the ground wire is already finished, in the absence of drying; the living room is clear so that the walls can be painted and everything is properly covered so that nothing is stained when painting. To be able to paint the next day, the team agrees that they could put heaters to accelerate the drying of the plaster of the walls. The Product Owner attends the Daily as a listener and communicates that, the same evening, the client will choose between the color samples that have been left on the wall.

In the fourth Daily the electrician announces that he has finished introducing the grounding and putting the plug where the music chain will go. The heaters have been put on all night and the wall is ready to be painted, because the plaster is already dry. The Product Owner announces that the client has already opted for a color, so everything is ready for the walls to be painted that same day.

The last day there is no Daily, because the team has finished with the Sprint Backlog, so they go directly to the Sprint Review. The team shows the painted walls and the plug, already with a ground connection included, to the Product Owner and the client. The color is just the one chosen by the client two days before and everything seems to be going well. The Product Owner plugs a radio player into the new plug, which is already grounded, to verify that it is working properly. They take advantage after the Sprint Review, to meet again and do a retrospective, and analyze if something could be improved. The Scrum Master facilitates the retrospective and appears with a wad of sticky notes and pens. The Scrum Master leaves them 5 minutes to write on the sticky notes what things have worked well and must be maintained. After spending 5 minutes, one by one gets up and exposes what they have written. In general, several agree that Scrum is working and must be maintained, and that the estimates have worked, since they have successfully completed the Sprint. Now the Scrum Master leaves them another 5 minutes to write down what things they think could be improved. After five minutes they stand up, one by one, to present the topics they think they could improve on. The following topics are discussed:

- The paintings were not bought.

- They started the work without the client having chosen the color.

They analyze each topic and reach the following conclusions:

- Buy the paintings before and add them to the budget. They can even ask the client for some money in advance to go sourcing the material.

- Do not wait so late for the client to choose the color he wants, as this affects the supply of material.

The team is already good in itself, but, from now on, it will be even better, because it has learned from its mistakes and has spoken openly and transparently.

The reason they write the topics in private, using sticky notes, is so they do not influence each other. If they were exposing the topics out loud, they would influence each other and, in the end, they would all end up exposing the same topics.

In the next Sprint it is only necessary to fix the floor, a task that is already estimated. Learning from the above mistakes, the Product Owner is concerned about talking to the client, so that he can choose the type of floor he wants to put on. That way they can collect parquet boards and have them before starting the Sprint. They also ask for an advance to the client, to buy material, as was discussed in the retrospective.

15.6 Sprint 2

The Backlog of Sprint 2 was already clear and it was even estimated, so the team starts to fix the parquet. To do this the floor has to be transparent, so all the furniture in the living room has to be moved. In the first Daily this is the conclusion they come to and the team starts up. In this way it is possible to take advantage of the electrician, the mason and the painter, who were not going to take part in the arrangement of the floor.

The day after clearing the room the floor is already laid and varnished. It has arrived in time, the team has optimized its resources and knows its Velocity: about 30 story points per Sprint. During the Sprint Review, the client is shown the finished room.

Conclusion

We have taken a trip through the Scrum framework, learning what it is and what its associated vocabulary is. Why does it work? We have seen that commitment comes from involvement. Although it is a principle that is not stated in the existing literature on Scrum, all the meetings prescribed by Scrum are tremendously participatory for the team, so the commitment of this is being achieved. The power that gives the commitment of a whole team is tremendous. It took me ten years to understand this. I was always surprised at how easy it was to get high-performance teams with Scrum, but I did not understand until I came across the work of Stephen Covey (Covey, 2013).

The companies that have applied it have revolutionized the Market with innovative ideas. It is not the same to have a specialist thinking about new solutions than to have a team of 9 members fully committed and with total freedom to speak. With so many members really committed, what one doesn't figure out, another one figures it out. And above, surrounded by an environment of respect and trust, the team grows to see that any idea is welcome and applied. That is the secret of Scrum.

Apart from this primordial secret, Scrum prescribes not to waste time on things that do not add value (enunciated as one of the principles of the Agile Manifesto), and stresses uses that are connatural to the human being:

- The estimate by comparison, for example.

- The use of information radiators, such as Kanban panels, to make it very clear what the team is working on.

Antonio Montes Orozco

- The awareness that we must maintain sustainable work rhythms (enunciated as another of the principles of the Agile Manifesto), so as not to burn the team and to maintain creativity, apart from reducing errors.

- The ability to learn from mistakes and apply continuous improvement (*Kaizen*, remember?) as a usual practice (enunciated as another principle of the Agile Manifesto, in relation to retrospectives).

We have also seen that Scrum is not the panacea, and that it is suitable for environments where teamwork is important, and where fixed duration iterations can be established and commitments cannot be changed. If the environment is very volatile and you cannot respect the work committed in each Sprint, Scrum limps, because that prevents from obtaining the Velocity of the team and make it predictable. For those cases, it is better to apply other agile methodologies, such as Kanban, for example.

Arriving at the end of this trip, I would like to have helped you learn about Scrum and how it applies. I wish you the best in your professional career and that this is full of success.

Antonio Montes Orozco

Information sources

Links of interest

- Agile Manifesto: http://agilemanifesto.org

- Agile Principles: http://agilemanifesto.org/principles.html

- About Maslow's Hierarchy of Needs: https://en.wikipedia.org/wiki/Maslow%27s_hierarchy_of_needs

- About Abraham Maslow: https://en.wikipedia.org/wiki/Abraham_Maslow

- About Theories X and Y of Douglas McGregor: https://en.wikipedia.org/wiki/Theory_X_and_Theory_Y

- About Theory Z: https://en.wikipedia.org/wiki/Theory_Z

- About Patrick Lencioni: https://en.wikipedia.org/wiki/Patrick_Lencioni

Recommended Books

- Adkins, L. (2010). *Coaching Agile Teams: A Companion for ScrumMasters, Agile Coaches, and Project Managers in Transition.* Pearson Education/Addison Wesley Professional

- Anderson, D. J. (2010). *Kanban: Successful Evolutionary Change for your Technology Business.* Blue Hole Press.

Antonio Montes Orozco

- Cockburn, A. (2000). *Agile Software Development: The Cooperative Game*. Pearson Education.

- Cohn, M. (2006). *Agile Estimating and Planning*. Pearson Education/ Addison Wesley Professional.

- Cohn, M. (2006). *User Stories Applied: For Agile Software Development*. Pearson Education.

- Covey, S. R. (2013). *The 7 Habits of Highly Effective People*. Simon & Schuster; Anniversary edition.

- Derby E., Larsen, D., Schwaber, K. (2006). *Agile Retrospectives: Making Good Teams Great*. Pragmatic Bookshelf.

- Hammarberg, M. (2014). *Kanban In Action*. Manning Publications.

- Highsmith, J. (2009). *Agile Project Management: Creating Innovative Products*. Pearson Education/Addison Wesley Professional

- Lencioni, P. (2002). *The Five Dysfunctions of a Team*. Jossey-Bass.

- Maslow, A. (2013). *A Theory of Human Motivation*. Martino Fine Books

- McGregor, D. (2006). *The Human Side Of Enterprise*. McGraw-Hill Education.

- Rawsthorne, D. (2011). *Exploring Scrum: The Fundamentals*. CreateSpace Publishing.

- Shalloway, A., Beaver, G., Trott J. R. (2009). *Lean-Agile Software Development*. Pearson Education.

Antonio Montes Orozco

- Sliger, M., Broderick, S. *The Software Project Manager's Bridge to Agility*. Pearson Education.

- Sutherland, J. (2014). *Scrum, The Art Of Doing Twice the Work in Half the Time*. Cornerstone Digital.

- Wysocki, R. K. (2009). *Effective Project Management: Traditional, Agile, Extreme*. Wiley.

Recommended articles

- Mathew Ricard, Antoine Lutz. *Mind of the Meditator*. Scientific American. No. 311 (November 2014).

- Robert Stickgold. *Beyond Memory: The Benefits of Sleep*. Scientific American. No. 313 (October 2015).

- Schwaber K. & Sutherland J. (2011). *The Scrum Guide*.

Special thanks

This section of the books has always caught my attention. The author gives a string of names that I don't know. Now that I have faced my first book, I have realized how hard it is to write a book and, when exceptional professionals and great friends help you, the truth is that you feel an infinite gratitude. How are you not going to dedicate a few words to people so endearing that have supported you in something as complicated as publishing a book? And in what order do I do it, if all the help has been exceptional?

I will do it in alphabetical order. I'll start with Angela and her wonderful English translation of this work. All my love also for Pilar, who, with great patience, has read the chapters and has given me some fabulous ideas. My thanks to Ramón and the piece of cover he has designed for the book. I cannot forget about Rocío, with her correct and wise corrections. You are a diamond in the rough, Roci. All my love for my indefatigable companion, Rosa. I have discovered in her a formidable editor and corrector of style. My thanks to Susana, who has always believed in me and gave me the facilities of Indizen Corporation to promote my book. Last, but not least, is Yolanda, with her amazing review of the English version. I am eternally grateful to all of them.

Antonio Montes Orozco

About the Author

Antonio Montes Orozco was born in Madrid, Spain, in 1972. He studied Telecommunications Engineering at the Polytechnic University of Madrid.

He began his first steps in the world of work as a systems administrator, specializing in the Solaris, HPUX and AIX operating systems. After a few years as a systems administrator, he started programming in C++ and, in 2006, he learned about the Scrum methodology and was one of the pioneers in its application in Spain. Since then he has been working as a Scrum Master and as a coach to implement this methodology.

He ended up working in a major Spanish financial institution, where he introduced Scrum in one of the Business areas.

He was certified in 2015 by the prestigious PMI (Project Management Institute), as a practitioner of agility (ACP: Agile Certified Practitioner), and by Scrum Manager in 2014.

In 2016 he obtained the Executive Master in Management of Information Technologies, by the Institute of Business Executives (IDE-CESEM) of Spain.

Antonio Montes Orozco

Credits

Scrum for Non-Techies: Learn how to use in your Business the methodology that led Google, Amazon, Facebook, Microsoft, and Lockheed Martin to success.

Antonio Montes Orozco

First edition in electronic book: January 2019

ISBN: 9781794046610

www.ingramcontent.com/pod-product-compliance
Lightning Source LLC
Chambersburg PA
CBHW051058050326
40690CB00006B/759